100 YEARS
LIFE SKETCH

Pathway to Spiritual Journey

Prof. Somraj Arya M. A., Ph. D.

Printed in the United States of America.

ISBN: 978-1-4907-1959-7 (sc)
ISBN: 978-1-4907-1961-0 (hc)
ISBN: 978-1-4907-1960-3 (e)

Library of Congress Control Number: 2013920865

Trafford rev. 11/26/2013

 www.trafford.com

North America & international
toll-free: 1 888 232 4444 (USA & Canada)
fax: 812 355 4082

*Dedicated to my father, Late Shri
Piara Lal Arya and my readers*

*A Perfect Gift to Donate or Recommend
to your family members, friends, staff,
well-wishers and Church members.*

Prof. Somraj Arya M. A., Ph. D.

A Prayer!

I pray to creator of this universe, the Lord,
has many names but still one Almighty God!
You are Master who give us life and breath,
and still controller of our births and death!
To you, no one could ever able to describe,
still all believe your presence and subscribe!
You said, if two or more together will pray,
you promise to be present, accept and obey!
With my father's soul; lying in your kingdom
and family, I request you grant me wisdom!
Let me recall dad's hymn, recite as he would,
I used to enjoy at most during my childhood!
By using those hymns, few verse from Book,
let me create for human, "Life Sketch" book!
Let me peep and watch your creative actions,
human feelings, behavior & social reactions!
Give me power that I should not write wrong,
I pray to the Almighty God, to whom I belong!
Let this sketch of human's life be all truthful,
the readers to accept You and remain faithful!

A Tribute To Woman!

God created two great things on this earth,
first the nature and second woman is worth!
She brings to world, our sisters and brothers,
to raise them properly, God made mothers!
A symbol of sacrifice, patience and support,
she take care of family and provide comfort!
She is powerful to hold the little kids in arm,
feeding and raising wisely give lion's form!
At bed during night, if her flesh pee and cry,
she herself lays on wet and put kids on dry!
As she opens mouth, she speaks in wisdom,
make others happy and still proud at none!
No doubt that in all matters she is a smart,
how to convince others, she has great art!
Treating husband as King, is usual process,
and treat children, like a prince or princess!
Don't treat her as a slave or a thing of lust,
remember her sacrifice, must give respect!

This is a truth and fact, don't make a mess,
always woman is behind, a man's success!
Yes, it is difficult to find a virtuous woman,
if found, is precious than diamond's crown!
By nature, she does her every best as wife,
and remains faithful till the end of her life!
In ease, she is nice, simple and just a plain,
if in anger, has powers to crush mountain!
She is beauty of nature, brighter than gold,
usually become mature after forty year old!
If stand by husband will receive His Grace,
don't be upset, just assist with smiling face!

First Year

You came to this world, sucking thumb[1]
giving pains to mother, while in womb!
For excitement and lust created by Him,
to continue the universe and not to dim!
The creator gave you this auspicious life,
for the keen desire of husband and wife!
Through their excite and the vital flood[2],
He made your features, veins and blood!
You, being a proof of your parent's love,
keep in mind, world also need your love!
Relative are happy to see and feel proud,
many people came to see you in crowd!
Remember to reap same what you seed,
and will be judged by Him, for your deed!
Just like parents, you have to play a part,
and you must become one, not to apart!
Keep remembering Him, although in brief,
this must be done, if want to avoid grief!

---

[1] **Thumb:** Usually the position of fetus in stomach is reversely
     hanged and sucking of thumb.
[2] **Vital flood:** Excreted fluid of human being.

Second Year

Second year came full of attractions,
and you are still getting affections!
Never forget and always remember,
love you get from all family member!
You were hanged in reverse[1] inside,
before you come the world outside!
Your mother suffered a lots of pains,
while was inside her belly and veins!
Her raising efforts, all night and day,
do not forget, debt you need to pay!
When was inside, parents had dream,
don't let them down, both had seen!
And don't forget that from the drops[2],
you are result of prayers and hopes!
They did their best and raised you up,
take care of them, when you grow up!
Remember suffering of your parents,
respect them before worship of God!

---

[1] **Reverse:** Position of fetus in stomach is reversely hanged and sucking of thumb.

[2] **Drops:** Excreted fluid of human.

Third Year

You entered in third year's immense,
with a great outlook and innocence!
You don't know anything good or bad,
if food is late, you easily become mad!
Want all siblings and parent's embrace,
if it is not there you annoyed to craze!
Like a king you want everyone's boss,
and yet unaware to any profit or loss!
You are very attractive just like a bud,
a lovely lotus coming out of the mud!
Always dressed up have excellent look,
like new cover of Bible; The Holy Book!
You always love to get everyone's kiss,
and your life to each is like a real bliss!
Always you just want to play and play,
remember that all is subject to decay!
Although it is good to play and smile,
remember it's not immortal but a while!

Fourth Year

Entered in the fourth, swings of moods,
mom gives you always delicious foods!
Know nothing except playing n sleeping,
that is the beauty of life you are keeping!
You are unaware of anything at this time,
thinking of sweet orange, could be lime!
Unaware what could happen any time,
not always true, that you think of mine!
The joy of small steps your parents get,
but your sudden fall make them upset!
Always remember, it's a universal truth,
innocence is faded by arrival of youth!
Both working hard to keep your smile,
don't give them later, pains of exile!
Must love your parent as they love you,
for judgment day, will be looked at too!
Keep in mind so that later don't repent,
for noble causes, you have been sent!

Fifth Year

Now that you entered in the fifth year,
no knowledge of the strangers or dear!
Still you enjoy different swing of moods,
crying for sweets and delicious foods!
You forgot to whom you came apart,
never worshiped, from core of heart!
Powerful kings and queens have gone,
you have to face Him one day as moan!
Time to come out of worldly pleasures,
remember you to face same measures!
Hard work of parents, be kept in mind,
never discard them and always be bind!
Keep in mind and be out of worldly net,
your ultimate goal is eternal life to get!
Remember the truth that rise has to fall,
the reality and universal law says it all!
Be faithful as all are the people of God,
make'em happy and never raise sword!

Sixth Year

You entered in sixth year jumping at max,
and if become tired, you lay down to relax!
Now you are enjoying the love of others,
never forget Him, His sons, your bothers!
All you learned is laughing and just laying,
if upset during play, you just start crying!
Now you know what is fantasy or reality,
and like to be with yours gender identity!
Also learning to make new connections,
know feelings, thoughts and reactions!
Learning new way of inventing n initiating,
started solving problems or just creating!
You just want to be the winner for royalty,
when angry, have no mercy or the loyalty!
You being the center of yours own invent,
punish[1] others for wrong, is the only intent!
It's time to think and accept your own fault,
so that at judgment, you don't feel a guilt!

---

[1] **Punish:** An act of slap during childhood when other create disturbance during play.

Seventh Year

In seventh years stop sleep, be awoke,
so that later you should not be broke!
He gave you windows of world to see,
took it granted, never tried to foresee!
Now you have forgot to remember Him,
who brought you in this earth kingdom!
He gave you the tongue to speak sweet,
be respectful to others, smile and greet!
You got ear to listen thought of wisdom,
but did not bothered and used it seldom!
To control others[1] you got a gift of brain,
to show them way, lead and to maintain!
Many left this world with a broken heart,
but you never felt feeling of being depart!
Now you are just clean, pure and innocent,
remember to mend ways, later not repent!
It is still time to remember and to get cure,
if not then later, you will become impure!

---

[1]   **Control Others:** As per belief, God gave brain and wisdom to
      human to control and maintain all other living being on earth.

Eighth Year

In your eighth year, you need to rise,
think the purpose of life and be wise!
Don't leave world empty in the proud,
be brave, strong n stand above crowd!
Without wisdom human is like a wild,
be capable, not like an average child!
Through work hard, you will be wise,
remember sky is limit, if want to rise!
Keep in mind, practice makes perfect,
remember it is true and also correct!
Work hard is the only key to success,
if managed wrong, you will in duress!
Make proper plans and keep an indent,
you need to know, Lincoln[1] President!
Don't ever try to lead life of a layman,
good dreaming, bring success to man!
Why don't you dream of heaven's gate,
still you have time and you aren't late!

---

[1]   **President Lincoln:** Abraham Lincoln. (See page 115)

Ninth Year

Wake up, stop sleeping in the ninth,
will be in loss while laying on berth!
Remember that you are not forever,
make best use of time, become clever!
Gone are those, who lived in flowers,
took bath in fountains and showers!
Gone are those eating costly muffins,
they left world even without coffins!
Great kings having many servants,
died all alone by the cut of serpents!
Gone is Rawan[1] and proudy Hitler[2],
today, no one can find their glitter!
Where is beautiful queen Mumtaj[3],
and builder of world's wonder Taj[4]!
Where to find Dashrath's son Rama[5],
forced to go jungle in family drama!
Gone are Mughals[6] had many wives,
who never showed pity in their life!

[1-6]   Please see appendix page at the end of this book.

Tenth Year

You have entered into the tenth year,
remember, life is short n have a fear!
You got a good and attractive body,
remember won't last long oh buddy!
You are enjoying world tours in bright,
never thought about wrong and right!
Eating delicious breads with the butter,
time will come, you may die in mutter!
If you don't take care of your endure,
result you may get may be of failure!
Ruining the temple of God is not good,
drug will finish you like worms of wood!
For intoxications, you are gone O boss,
you will never be able to recover loss!
To help the needy you became a miser,
but still you consider yourself a wiser!
Sons of same God we all are brothers,
born to die, why do you bother others!

11th Year

Now you have entered in eleventh year,
and feeling proud in company of other!
Enjoying the cools and life's pleasures,
a time will come to leave this Oh dear!
Today you have all pleasures and joy,
if won't have teeth, no food to enjoy!
All your saluters will be gone brother,
so be nice and polite towards other!
You won't have forever all official rank,
so be nice to all, before become crank!
Soon great books will go to drawers,
still is time to read them and admire!
No smell of perfume will last forever,
except the good deeds to live forever!
All of friends will go away from you,
it's right time you must enjoy it now!
Moon will go soon and will not glow,
so look at the sky and enjoy it now!

12th Year

Entering in twelfth is puberty's trends,
spending time in opposite sex friends!
If you think that they are your for sure,
please be advised that this is not true!
Enjoying cuisines, costly food and spoon,
friends will leave you, if money is gone!
Skipping from school for the sake of peer,
your life won't be good, listen it my dear!
Friends are nothing, just getting the flair,
if they find better, for sure will go there!
Until certain time, everything looks good,
please use your own wisdom, if you could!
Going against nature, brings destruction,
be advised and have a solid construction!
Obey your teachers to make the progress,
and parents dream shouldn't be in duress!
The path that go towards Church, is right,
get rid of dark, and enjoy heaven's light!

13th Year

Thirteenth is same sisters n brothers,
leave proud and adamant, to others!
You don't bother if it is a day or night,
want to rise high and high like a kite!
Why you do not listen advises of elder,
this is the only way to make life better!
Remember it is time to be more careful,
be good in behavior, nice and faithful!
Do not run away from Church or Dom,
listen to your priest, father and Mom!
If you will listen to their good advice,
it will make your life happy and nice!
Doing bad in the name of fun and Joy,
will ruin your body and life will destroy!
Leave bad habits of drinking and drugs,
you must go to priest to get nice hugs!
Visit your church on the regular driven,
will take you to salvation and heaven!

14th Year

Now you entered in fourteenth year,
still not attained wisdom, my dear!
Got attracted to blue, jazz and pops,
and in excitement, waste vital drops!
Go to school and continue for learning,
for your bad deeds will make it burning!
Use your tongue for the sweet word,
do not make others bad and absurd!
Give food to eat to hard working labor,
do not snatch ever, the fruits of other!
Don't just show to hold The Holy Book,
make progress, do not become crook!
God want you to be nice to the other,
don't be harsh to your sister or brother!
You will be ruined by bad deed's curse,
to be saved, don't stop going to church!
He sent you to world for His internship,
it is still time to manage and worship!

15th Year

You entered in fifteenth year of your life,
but haven't started to think and be wise!
You can't be wiser, if skip classes in glad,
You cannot reap good, if sowed was bad!
How you can get food, if none was fed?
How can you be covered, if never covered?
How can you go heaven, if never obeyed?
You won't be secure, if never ever saved?
It will be difficult, when you become sick,
physician won't save you, when He click!
You have all pleasures and enough fame,
but one day people will forget your name!
You must know the truth, at your moan,
dears won't keep body, when you gone!
Wealth won't be of use, if you won't be,
don't disobey at all, if want Him to see!
Stop your ego, lust, greed and fake pride,
if you want to find Him, just look inside!

16th Year

Welcome to the sixteenth year of grace,
charming youth and glimpse on the face!
Mustache and beard make guys perfect,
youth of female also gets a huge attract!
Both are hallucinated, that none to watch,
and to fulfill the lust everyone is at catch!
Glowing from outside, but inside a wicked,
for sake of money, are ready to be picked!
Both like to wear rings, necklace and roam,
even not fully developed, and using foam!
Males are now guys, father became pop,
girls are now babes, and mother is mom!
To make a taller look, she wears pin heel,
and to make more glow, buying the peel!
Boy wear pants and jackets made of nike[1],
to show off body girls are riding the bike!
Sitting with friends, drink Chivas[2] in cheers,
to girls wine or beer is good in the peers!

---

[1]   **Nike:** A famous brand name for apparel. (See page 123)
[2]   **Chivas:** A branded Whisky (See page 116)

Everyone at peak looking to enjoy the max,
always searching the opposite just for sex!
To get into opposite, started doing all odds,
crazy mind need by hook or crook methods!
All are going far away from the good deed,
ready to do anything, just to fill the need!
Lost family values, forgot elder's respect,
their religion is now-a-days only the lust!
Becoming outlaw and are just blind in lust,
with "First Site Love[1]" title, smashing trust!
Both became deaf, stopped listening advice,
all are just doing, whatever to them is nice!
Please become wise and find the real portal,
always worship God if want to be immortal!

---

[1] **First Site Love or Love at First Sight:** General conception of passionate love or a kind of madness. Now-a-days sometimes this is used by young male and or female to fulfill lust, defraud and exploit others.

17th Year

You entered seventeenth years of accord,
and have completely forgotten the God!
You started and enjoying wine and beer,
babes n guys enjoying together in cheer!
If the lust is at extreme and becomes due,
satisfy it or just go to watch movie in blue!
Age is not big deal for you to do fun or sex,
somehow get someone to enjoy it at max!
Any one is okay, your known or unknown,
you don't even bother, put blood to down!
As an excited horse wander here and there,
looking to fulfill lust with any youth mare!
Even kidnap of minor is okay to your trail,
you don't bother, even caught n sent jail!
Now you have forgot Bible's precious verse,
that cheating who trust you, is a big curse!
To fulfill the lust with anyone, is okay to you,
and all times sex is only main motive to you!

In the neighborhood, office or at work,
doesn't matter, if cashier, boss or clerk!
You never loose and miss any of chance,
for drinking, enjoying and of romance!
Babes with relative or friends of brother,
guys don't bother even age of a mother!
You came this world for service of God,
but due to lust, gone away from Lord!
Still it is a good time, life not to mess,
save from curse of hell, go and confess!

18th Year

Entered eighteenth, you are officially adult,
wandering sharp suited and looking for lust!
Wearing attractive glasses at public places,
beautifully dressed up, booted shiny laces!
To make impression, you rented costly cars,
and posing yourself, like came from mars!
Girls are acting to show them like as pure,
aren't faithful to one, though show endure!
Showing nice in talking and posing a truth,
in fact lying everywhere at school or booth!
Although you pose to look as gentleman,
but from inside, you are just wicked man!
Collecting wealth for opposite to attract,
thinking nothing, except sexual contract!
Started doing wrong, all odds and means,
oh look at even wearing a torn-out jeans!
By holding Bible nicely, covered in pearls,
usually girl search male and boys for girls!

19th Year

Now you entered in the nineteenth year!
you need to know truth of life my dear!
Wealth will not last . . . . . . .so donate it now!
Youth won't last long . . . . . make good now!
Name won't last. . . . . understand it now!
Soon eyes will shut. . . . . . enjoy nature now!
Tongue will stop . . . . .sing hymns now!
Teeth won't last . . . . give smile now!
Body will depart . . . . go to Church now!
Body is a machine. . . . . . . .overhaul it now!
Building will decay . . . . . . .give shelter now!
Fame won't last . . . . .so do good now!
Breath won't be more . . . . enjoy it now!
Life is short . . . . .live and let live now!
Born has to die . . . . understand it now!
Soul will depart . . . . read Bible now!
Want to be immortal? . . . . do good now!
Tomorrow will be late . . . . . .go Church now!

21st Year

You have entered in youth twenty-first year,
glow at face become attractive and clear!
Glowing mustaches gives an attractive look,
still looking new ways for females to hook!
Always standing at the mirrors with thought,
what to do, to become more n more smart!
Your look is perfect like a bright sun of noon,
shining like stars around, midnight's moon!
You wearing new, bright and costly Jacket,
so that opposite can come to you in attract!
Being at youth your pride is now at its top,
you don't like those, look poor or at a slop!
You have joined gym just to look in powers,
spray costly perfumes instead of showers!
The way you are indulged in the bad deed,
your forefather's glory is going to be fade!
Still time, be careful before you go to God,
later it will be difficult to please the Lord!

22nd Year

While you are in year of twenty second,
forgotten fact of life that death is end!
Youth is short lived; it is just as simple,
it will go away while fading of pimple!
So, inclined towards the chosen friend,
don't want to leave, neither to mend!
You have created a new style of walk,
those, who look poor, you don't talk!
To show off your power, and its peak,
you beat the beast or even the weak!
If the beloved is away, nothing is right,
you become furious and ready to fight!
You stopped to listening elder's advice,
if they insist, you do make fun of these!
You discard Him and busy with female,
your soul n God, like water and whale!
It is high time that you mend your way,
confess and start good, before decay!

23rd Year

Now you entered in twenty-third year,
but you don't think of to be wise dear!
Having seen people leaving the world,
but still you are not upset or worried!
Your body is strong, powerful norms,
will be eaten up by the earth worms!
When soul will go, body to get death,
it will be just flesh, without a breath!
No more shopping at the great malls,
will be of no use, the beautiful walls!
Soon beauty and body will be gone,
people will forget you and will moan!
Family will not wait to keep the body,
still time to donate wealth, to needy!
Wealth will be useless and in its total,
if you donate, may become immortal!
Still you have time, confess your sins!
start going Church for worship wins!

24th Year

Twenty fourth year now you got,
to go to Church, still not thought!
You are engaged in fulfilling lust,
won't get heaven, need to trust!
Now you are in peak and anger,
if will not stop, will be in danger!
In hallucination, that it is bright,
going to the wrong not to right!
Those are great, who stick to one,
each is for one, not for everyone[1]!
The God creates and she bears[2],
lots of pains to bring, oh dear!
Think her efforts, for you to raise[3],
don't insult, you need to praise!
Except spouse you must treat,
her sister or mother and greet!
Listen with ears, truth of a tale,
He will greet, if respect female!

---

[1] **Everyone:** Physical relations should not be developed
     with everyone.
[2] **Bears:** Bearing of pains at the time of birth.
[3] **Raise:** Efforts to raise a child.

25th Year

Ah! youthful twenty five entered,
war on lust, yet to be conquered!
You wasted one fourth of your life!
stick each other, husband and wife!
Left the parents and came as bind,
now over small things, don't grind!
Took oath to bind, in heart you did,
now be happy, and raise little kid!
You don't break marriage, oh duffer,
for your fault, why your kids suffer!
From top to bottoms, all are same,
newer is nothing, do not be insane!
Prost for wealth, in count of push,
to get you in, just beating the bush!
Listen advise, it is hard to find neat,
stick to your own, don't be in cheat!
Book says, two to become one flesh,
don't sin against self, life will mess!

26th Year

Welcome to the twenty-sixth year,
death is certain, but you unaware!
Now you do not want dust to touch,
left is few to soiled, not that much!
Now wear soft cloths, high in cost,
making soul dirty, going to prost!
Not be indulged, in all fake trend,
you may not get, a coffin in end!
At end, won't be saved by doctor,
will be looked by deed, character!
Just for the sake of your all action,
bad health in end will be reaction!
Seek advice of astrologer to solicit,
when end will come can't predict!
You will not be healed, or be cured
unless you worship the Holy Lord!
Without the grace of the Almighty,
you are nothing, don't be naughty!

27th Year

In twenty-seven, you are a traitor,
have forgotten your God, Creator!
At peak and pride of your youth,
has already ruined your mouth!
You think yourself just like a king,
but are unaware that you a bing!
You always fit of sexual thoughts,
drink wine, eat meat in draughts!
Because of your so-called proud,
good virtues are melted in cloud!
Treating bad father and mothers,
you forgot how to respect others!
Being indulged in all the bad deed,
uneducated, forgot Book to read!
Forgot creator, who gave you all,
you will be audited, to explain all!
To get rid and be saved from pain,
still it is good time you to abstain!

28th Year

Now you are in twenty eighth,
but in Him, don't have a faith!
You are spoiled, not for creed,
and you are ruined in bad deed!
Never gave to poor even a dime,
and showed pride all the time!
To show off the false succeeds,
you driving rented mercedes[1]!
You used odd means for wealth,
wasting in bad, ruining health!
Due to odd deeds you will go jail,
other's efforts may come on bail!
You are fond of to eat costly food,
feeding others, is not in the mood!
While drinking at clubs in night,
if other look at yours, you fight!
Just be advised, its give and take,
relations look real, but is a fake!

---

[1] **Mercedes:** Mercedes-Benz is a multinational German manufacturer of luxury car.

Fake relation, of aunty and aunts,
may bring bad name and taunts!
You are unable to think the logic,
don't know His glory and magic!
Do whatever of interest to you,
keep in mind to go to Him, too!
By looking at what you did bad,
He will throw you in hot n sand!
Still time to get apply His advise,
go to Church and become a wise!

29th Year

Although twenty-ninth has came,
you still in illusions of fake fame!
Remember truth, later don't cry,
whosoever has born, has to die!
Where is beauty queen Mumtaj[1]
Shah Jahan[2] who made the Taj[3]!
Where are the kings with crowns,
had inscribed their name on coins!
Where is proudy Hitler[4] or Akbar[5],
great figures of history and other!
George[6], Henry[7] or other big name,
All have gone, that ruled the Spain!
Where is Boudica[8] or King Herod[9],
or the Wrights[10], Newton[11] or Ford[12]!
They all have gone and so will you,
this is reality you should mind too!
Stop thinking of pride and fame,
be serious and believe His name!

[1-12]   Please see appendix pages in the end of this book.

30th Year

Having entered thirtieth of age,
remember that the life is a stage!
Pride will go away, if you ready,
happiness to come, if you ready!
You can not see all the sufferings,
if you don't try to look from top?
You can never become a humble,
until you do not come to a slope!
How can you become a pure one,
if you are not nice to the others!
You will never get praised at all,
If you don't respect your mother!
How can you know the real value,
of hunger, til you are worthy rich!
How can you enjoy the true love,
until to your own, you don't stick!
How you can you meet Almighty,
until you don't follow His path?

31st Year

Having entered thirty first of age,
but you are still acting like craze!
He gave you precious life, in trust,
you never obeyed, that was must!
He sent you to sing the holy song,
but you started doing the wrong!
Remember, you won't be a hero,
soon breath stock will be the zero!
Plane of life is flying at speed fast,
and destination is at point of last!
To whom you raised in your arm,
will burry in ground, if not warm!
To whom you used to give muffin,
will wrap the body in white coffin!
Whom you used to sing for sleep,
if left no money, they won't weep!
Be wise and start going to Church,
enjoy Creator's company forever!

32nd Year

You entered in thirty second year,
still unaware of the audit, my dear!
You have completely forgotton God,
what will be reply, if asked by Lord!
Now you are always in pride at full,
having power of wealth, pity at null!
These will be your main causes to fell,
Don't go by me, The Holy Bible to tell!
You always rude and cruel to other,
none can save you my dear brother!
Bad deeds will bring insult, not lore,
you won't have a respect anymore!
It is the time to start speaking sweet,
so that you should be loved and greet!
Listen carefully, the priest's preaching,
want die in peace, obey His teaching!
If will do this, sure you will be seated,
in God's Heaven and will be greeted!

33rd Year

By entering into thirty-third year,
and have enjoyed enough my dear!
Now you enjoyed much of steaks,
youthful smiling lips and cheeks!
Many times visited prost's gates[1]
enjoyed beds with house maids!
Crushed buds, without any tension,
under shining lights[2] of mansions!
You have enjoyed all of comforts,
yelled for nothing at your servants!
Been gifted with the kids around,
harshly shouts, not sweet sound!
Having enjoyed the parks at walks,
spending richly, was town's talks!
You never liked, holy song or hymn,
have interest in jazz like a demon!
Still time, get escaped from pain,
must stop doing bad, be abstain!

---

[1] **Prost's gate:** Prostitute's House
[2] **Mansions:** Large and impressive house

34th Year

Now you thirty-fourth old,
still ego is not controlled!
Think what you want to be
a good person or the bad?
Think what you want to be
a religious or the evil one?
A donator or miser person?
A dull or as a wiser person?
An honest person or a thief?
Want to be happy or in grief?
A humble or just a dictator?
A nice person or a traitor?
A normal, loved by many?
A true friend or an enemy?
Keep in mind that you are,
what you think, you are!
That is the way to go and,
that is what it should be!

35th Year

Now is thirty-fifth to mention,
but not thinking of salvation!
Listen carefully and just hold,
all that glitters may not gold!
Ears will not be able to knew,
and teeth won't be to chew!
Soon eyes won't able to see,
patella may keep jam knee!
Stomach may not be to digest,
breath will end, that is must!
Your youth will go very fast,
shine will not forever to last!
Now is the time to donate,
so that you should be given!
Now is time to love others,
so that you should be loved!
Whosoever come, has to go,
it happened to all, so be you!

36th Year

Now you are thirty-sixth,
pride and greed are mix!
Much inclined to the lust,
to safe, you leave must!
You got enough but still,
you are not contented!
You pose to be genuine,
but are an opportunist!
You show off as sincere,
but cheating to spouse!
Pretend to be spiritual,
but ghost[1] from inside!
Whom do you deceive,
and pose be different!
Don't you know that,
the God knows this all?
Don't try as can't hide,
as He is watching you!

---

[1]   **Ghost:** Spirit or soul of a dead person (see page 116)

37th Year

Your thirty-seventh has brought,
the bad deeds and evil thought!
Bad behavior that you treating,
messing up yourself in cheating!
Even if you have enough wealth,
will not save, when in ill health!
Kill bad thought and playing foul,
don't make yourself like evil soul!
All are equal, don't make a mess,
red blood, bones and same flesh!
Don't differentiate in big or small,
for wealth will not go along at all!
Don't differentiate in praying mod,
all are the ways to reach the God!
Believe in Him and don't be upset,
if fall, He will make you stand up!
Trust in the God and do the right,
be advised, your future is bright!

38th Year

Thirty-eight year has came,
don't sleep to get a shame!
Don't be lazy and unaware,
remember that God is there!
Get rid of your all bad deed,
put Him first, besides need!
Time is running at a speed,
think about Him, pay heed!
Sure you need Lord's bless,
without it, won't get access!
If you don't, will put to fire,
still time, start Him admire!
Later you will curse the fate,
when He will close His gate!
Just worship is key to success
and this is truth not a guess!
If you don't leave the proud,
remember, will be deprived!

39th Year

In thirtyninth, you well dressed,
continuing sins, not confessed!
Making mansions like big fort,
many are there just to escort!
Horses, forces, will not prevail,
will not save you from a devil!
Nice fountains, carpets or lawn,
you won't enjoy this at a dawn!
Now warehouse is full of grain,
will not last long and will drain!
You have never feed any hungry,
sure you are, making Him angry!
Not donating to those who need,
you are not rich, a poor indeed!
Don't proud to fill lust with poor,
you will be judged, that is sure!
Want to be with Him, leave pride,
start worshipping and do right!

40th Year

Look the fortieth year came fast,
just like a coast to coast Amtrak[1]!
Big portion of the breath stocks,
making empty godown and pots!
Youth is gone, old age is behind,
like dark is waiting noon to end!
Days, weeks, months and year,
making life short, make it clear!
Stop playing frauds and deceit,
must listen to, what says priest!
Snatching from poor who need,
filling your drums with a greed!
Why do not you listen my dear,
that your end time is very near!
Now is time start mending way,
no one can save you to decay!
If really want to be immortal,
then Almighty God is the portal!

---

[1]   **Amtrack:** US fast railroad passenger train.

41st Year

Now forty first year of life has come,
keep in mind that you will be gone!
Roots with God, but you are in grief,
you are just stem, without any leaf!
If still not awake, then will be in loss,
wake up now get rid of sleep Oh Boss!
You enjoyed world, got enough fame,
it is time to think, where from came!
He won't bother, how rich you were,
will be of concern, how poor you are!
You are well read by attending school,
without Holy Bible, you are just stool!
Poor gets greet and richer to be slain,
as rich do sins but poor are just plain!
Brave kings and rulers won't at nitch,
He won't care, even if they were rich!
Wealthy persons and owners of mall,
will go to Hell, for not worship at all!

42nd Year

The forty second year is running like train,
remember all the time won't be the same!
You are keeping records of what you made,
but never thought of loss of many decade!
Day-night consuming, 24K breaths Oh boss,
but you never bothered about precious loss!
Now that you are careless, later if request,
won't be listened for, a few more breath!
If want long life, work and relax[1] the max,
managing, may get 100 years plus excess!
Double[2] to be consumed in stress and grief,
remember these will shortening life in brief!
Using drugs n excite, wasting six[3] and plus,
making your life nothing else but just mess!
Eat proper and holding of yoga[4] will shade,
you to live long a century plus two decade!
To get eternity of life and your final portal,
you need to worship to become immortal!

---

[1] **Relax:** To make less tense or rigid
[2] **Double**: Breaths are consumed in double during stress and grief.
[3] **Six:** By consuming intoxication while in sex, breaths are
      consumed by six or more times.
[4] **Yoga:** A technique to keep health fit (see page 126)

43rd Year

By entering forty third, left with little to go,
still have not been able to control your ego!
Bad deeds made short, which was long call,
still time to do something, not be late at all!
Still time to negotiate, if you need mutation,
will seek from God, as He has your solution!
Give up business of bad deeds and be clever,
start doing good, make huge profit forever!
He said you will be forgiven, and it is a sure,
provided you are ready for it and do endure!
He will open door, but all you have to knock,
wake up and do worship, at speech of cock!
He will forgive you, if you are ready to repent,
but will be punished, if you act like a serpent!
Must need to worship and should have trust,
you will be with Him and won't be in the dust!
When, how much, and what is human's need,
He knows and will give, if you don't at greed!

44th Year

Ah! now that your entered in forty four,
keep in mind, life is not a long anymore!
You never ever sang hymns in His praise,
like lost tongue, became moan or craze!
Now you are not listening chanting bell,
if lost ears, dumb, will be thrown in hell!
Going for a Holy bath, just to show clean,
not outward shines, but inside, He mean!
Why treating female just as a tool of lust,
you came through her and need to respect!
Giving to needy or to those facing hardship,
remember that this is also a kind of worship!
In ego treating yourself like superior to all,
must keep remember that He is above all!
Your wisdom is ruined and you are a mad,
as can't make difference in good and bad!
Remember and not blame to the God at all,
that you have become, enemy of yourself!

45th Year

In forty fifth means about half is gone,
but still don't have Bible and are moan!
In madness, got enough worldly read,
nothing is that, which really you need!
You have discarded the real teachings,
and never listened priest's preaching!
Although you attended college classes,
but never have thought of life's losses!
You can't understand the real wisdom,
which can take you to God's Kingdom!
People who got the secrets, are numb,
remain silent and never beaten drum!
Always in the bed just to fulfill the lust,
know reality of life, understand must!
To have links with Him, you must care,
just simple life is best, not of pleasure!
Those are rich, who got riches of God
and always remain happy, in all mod!

It makes a noise, if the pot is an empty,
still and constant, are sign of His plenty!
Having established a deep link with Him,
are not of concern, if it is bright or dim!
Crowd in joy but in sorrow no one is near,
that is real proof of all the nears and dear!
Lust, greed, pride, anger and worldly fame,
are big enemies of humans, just to name!
Those who are always away from these,
have everlasting smiles and are in ease!
They don't care about the lust or greed,
are contented and nothing they need!
Love gets love, it's a universal truth dear,
will reap same as sowed, make it clear!
Good heart loves all and can never hate,
still time to think and should not be late!

46th Year

The forty six year of age has come,
the reality of life is short, be aware!
The Sun, Moon and Stars also obey,
all are there, and will never decay[1]!
They being with the God, are bright,
are giver to humanity in day n night!
Even cock[2] and sparrow[3] in the dawn,
pray to God, before they go to lawn!
Wild, beast and all living being pray,
better than human, because of obey!
Up in morning, thank Him and pray,
for taking care in night and next day!
Do good as you can during the day,
don't tease any and never foul play!
Don't forget pray, if don't want mess,
do work properly, to achieve success!
God has gave you precious human life,
if married, must pray along with wife!

---

[1] **Sun, Moon and Stars**: It is believed that Sun, Moon and Stars live forever as they obey God

[2] **Cock:** The early speech of cock is believed as worship of God

[3] **Sparrow:** The early speech of sparrow is believed as worship of God

47th Year

Forty seven year of your age has come,
still inclined to bad and good to none!
It will be difficult to enter into his ward,
until you are not ready and work hard!
To get Him your side, difficult to attain,
you will win for sure, if you make it aim!
If you really want to enjoy God's fruits,
you need not to be dressed up in suits!
Know how to win and fix eyes on target,
listen advice of priest and never forget!
Happiness is your right, that you should,
but record of your deeds must be good!
Everyone wants to go and enjoy heaven,
but you can't go, if worshiping demon!
Look, if you want to have fulfill appetite,
you need sing holy and hymns to recite!
Whosoever wants to go to the heaven,
then must not be afraid of the death!

48th Year

Although forty eight year has came,
but not started worshiping His name!
As you will go, sure you will be asked,
you did bad, why good was masked!
You will be asked, why created mess,
outside to be clean n inside ugliness!
Why terrified others, gave them pain,
why robbed them, it was not the aim!
You will be asked, if teased innocent,
at time you won't be able to repent!
He will ask you, why you not donated,
you were given to give, what created!
You will be punished, if not did well,
for not paying heed, to chant of bell!
You will be asked and cursed for sure,
why you had never helped any poor!
You will be cursed for not doing well,
as a punishment will be sent to hell!

49th Year

Your forty nine year of age has elapsed,
your precious portion has been collapsed!
You never worshiped, just spoiled your life,
never tried to find the God and ruined life!
Brave are those, who take care of the life,
they are enlightened and are not in grief!
Being contented, don't show, remain nice,
they do not just pretend, in fact are wise!
They don't roar of having attained the aim,
by doing all good, are winners of game!
Why doing bad and making life a difficult,
just worship with clean heart to see result!
Your own are selfish, its not good to sound,
they won't keep a night, soon will ground!
Pride, anger and greed, you need to throw,
all will be meaningless, once you will go!
Nothing will go with, so don't need to hold,
except the treasures of worshiping the God!

50th Year

The fifty year, middle of century came,
just like black hairs, soon will go name!
Black turned to white is an indication,
that he is calling you by this invitation!
Your degrees and diplomas are wasted,
if real joy and content was not tasted!
Educated is that . .who believe in God!
Educated is that . . who help the poor!
Educated is that . . . who love others!
Educated is that .who take life serious!
Educated is that . who care for others!
Educated is that . . . who never fights!
Educated is that . who show pity to all!
Educated is that . . . who don't pride!
Educated is that . . . who don't anger!
Educated is that . . who goes Church!
Educated is that . . . who love nature!
Real literate is one who trust Creator!

51st Year

The fifty first year of age is at host,
more than half of a century is lost!
Keep in mind that if you want light,
go to priest, he to show you bright!
He will show you reality and preach,
since, you don't know, he will teach!
Stop calculating and don't be a boss,
just trust Him, you won't be in loss!
The human is part of almighty God,
His part in human, so he is of Lord!
Keep in mind, not in hallucination,
Christianity based on incarnation!
Why go to others, if not have ticket,
safe journey to heaven is at a click!
You must be aware, shine will dim,
keys of heaven, just lies with Him!
Don't waste time, don't be apart,
want Him? need worship to start!

52nd Year

The fifty second year age has came,
still leading life, without Holy name!
Why you pose as knowledgeable lad,
without realizing, the good and bad!
You are aware, soul will leave soon,
still you are making yourself a fool!
Until you do not let yourself to bow,
doing wrong, will be continue to go!
Until you are not awake, can't start,
will face trouble if will remain apart!
Don't become of yourself an enemy,
only He is a friend, don't need many!
Until you leave bad and don't endure,
you will be in sorrow, won't be pure!
Parrot and beetle[1] story, good to read,
parrot lost eyes and also life indeed!
Understand what is real love, oh fool,
make your heart full of love, be cool!

---

[1]   **Parrot and Beetle:** An ancient story (see page 123)

53rd Year

By entering in the fifty third year song,
you have completed the journey long!
Teeth now started to fell down at most,
still you are hungry of the sex and lust!
All you have done bad at the extreme,
but now is the right time to improve!
It is time to wash yourself from inside,
do not just clean the dung at outside!
You have enjoyed the delicious sweets,
time to taste sour and see how treats!
You have enjoyed all comforts at most,
now is time to get ready for the worst!
Time has come for another tour to start,
that will take you to weakness toward!
This powerful body will not be any more,
if breaths are over, sickness won't cure!
Although you don't like ordinary beds,
will repent for past and tears to shed!

Your costly suits, that keep you warm,
will soon be eaten up by earth worm!
A beautiful deer caught up in the bush,
will struggle, to run away, in the rush!
Now that you are enjoying to see Moon,
at the fortnight's end, will go very soon!
You still have time, try and do your best
to enjoy His company, and Lap to rest!

54th Year

Now it is fifty fourth year at the trend,
a tornado has brought a strong wind!
Age is going like the clouds in the sky!
Age is going like a fast speedy boat!
Age is at speed like the water from top!
Age is going like smoke of the cloud!
Don't create problems for time to come,
start doing whatever is needed to done!
You completely ruined in ego and pride,
you do not know, what is good and bad!
You do not get in chained of fake love,
relations are for selfish, not any above!
Your hairs turning from black to white,
and future is all dark, not at all bright!
Get wisdom while you having strength,
don't wait, for end of your life's length!
So you forget past and start doing right,
so that after your end, future be bright!

55th Year

You are now in fifty five years of age,
still got caught in relationship's cage!
Never tried to make relation with God,
and never even tried to find the Lord!
Remember your path, need to hound,
and spiritualism, not easily be found!
Many of saints, claims to know Him,
its always not true, must dark or dim!
Those who has met Him are supreme,
God give wisdom of future in dream!
They are always happy in rain or shine,
Don't know difference in yours or mine!
They have lot of patience and don't cry,
even cut them into pieces, just to try!
No one can harm if inclined in moan,
because their pain sensors, are gone!
Even through the fire, come as brave,
The Jesus Christ, came out of grave!

56th Year

The fifty six year of age is coming but,
still sitting in pride and own ego's hut!
History tells us king of Ceylon[1] station,
pride ruined not just him, whole nation!
Until do not make your fake ego a dim,
won't go to heaven, won't be with Him!
It is good to accept Him, and be abide,
and get rid of your ego, also false pride!
Just devote yourself only to the greater,
The Almighty God the universe creator!
If you decided this, you won't in pride,
He will show you path, nothing to hide!
Where you learned of different game,
all are equal, as created by the same!
Same blood and bones, don't play foul,
all got equal sensors and same of soul!
If you trust Him, sure you will be saved,
otherwise you are just like an animal!

---

[1]   **King of Ceylone:** King Ravana also known as Rawan of Sri
Lanka (see page 124)

57th Year

The fifty seven year of age is coming,
still do not understood life's meaning!
Never knew your destination to reach,
and forgotten, what priest had teach!
Never tried to think or even imagine,
like shot of hunter's bullet on pigeon!
Not thought of back, where you shall,
never ever thought of the fire of hell!
You lost in worldly affairs, false chain,
and forgotten mission, that was main!
You never tried find fault, in yourself,
instead for greed, cursing poor wolf[1]!
Try to open His door, not everywhere,
because real happiness is just there!
You try to realize, what is your need,
its difficult to get, you must pay heed!
If you do not came out of yours ease,
you will never see His brightest light!

---

[1]   **Wolf:** An old story of wolf and Lion (see page 125)

58th Year

The fifty eight year age, still at the wait,
you have not thought, of end ultimate!
Saints of God in heaven, are enjoying,
but you will be in fire, why destroying!
Beloved of Lord are contented forever,
others will be restless, get peace never!
Wealthy are those, who do not love it,
curses to those, who always cry for it!
Of course they are away, from dwelling,
God give delicious food, in their shelling!
The beloved of God have great courage,
they don't proud and never discourage!
Whole world is full of blind, always cries,
except beloved of God, have divine eyes!
getting more than need is not authority,
the wealth, jewelry, or even the property!
The real happiness that beloved will enjoy,
has no comparison at all and never be any!

59th Year

Now fifty ninth of age at your hand,
you will face end, must understand!
Due to women, work and weather,
everyone is confused, my brother!
By holding gun, missiles and atom,
one nation want finish other nation!
Just open your eyes, see terrorism,
how world is filled up with egoism!
Some are upset for loss in the trade,
other are in loss for worldly shade!
Some upset because of depression,
others upset for global recession!
Economy is needed a fresh reboot,
rich want to finish poor from root!
Earlier king is responsible as main,
the newer will try to make it again!
His noble efforts, without any greed,
will make him a winner to succeed!

60th Year

Now sixty years of age is at fate,
still not thinking to become great!
Great are those who love others!
Great are those who do donate!
Great are those who don't cheat!
Great are those who go to Church!
Great are those who obey to Him!
Great are those who ready to go!
Be aware to be asked and cursed,
for false pride, you need to leave!
Be aware to be asked and cursed,
for false anger, you need to leave!
Be aware to be asked and cursed,
for teasing others, need to stop!
Be aware to be asked and cursed,
for cheating spouse, need to stop!
Only those will be rewarded, who
obey the teachings of Almighty God!

61st Year

In the sixty first, need to pay heed,
but still not ashamed of your deed!
Here buy home and becoming greedy,
there your grave is becoming ready!
Here using gel, new tools to shave,
there coffin is ready for your grave!
Here you are enjoying the gardens,
there journey is started by warden[1]!
Here as your heart will stop to pump,
there your body will soon be dump!
Summon is ready to appear to Him,
case will be decided when it is dim!
Sickness will become excuse of death,
when stock is at zero, of your breath!
Empty jaw, dim eyes, and no speech,
will be destination's tickets to reach!
Still you can make best use of time,
be routed to Church and the Lord!

---

[1]   **Warden:** The messenger of God

62nd Year

At sixty second, year need to trust,
it the time to leave hunger of lust!
It is okay if hunger of food, is much,
just work hard to, feed the stomach!
All are compelled to eat for reason,
all have to do, because of stomach!
Going one place to other, in search
of tasty foods, because of stomach!
Rich became poor and then went to,
beg at streets, because of stomach!
Everyone wants relax to the max,
but just can't because of stomach!
Birds are caught in the hunter's net,
just because of their own stomach!
You are cutting living being in pieces,
just because to feed yours stomach!
Sometimes kill others and do sins,
just because you got the stomach!

Sometimes you skipped the Church,
just because the hunger of stomach!
You can leave the wealth, but can't,
leave food, just because of stomach!
Some saints returned to world again,
just because that they got stomach!
Food is vital for stomach, fact to say,
God is vital for your soul, same way!
For soul's hunger, His refuge is best,
you won't feel any hunger or thirst!

63th Year

The sixty third of your age has come,
you are just motivated by the greed!
If you would not have the greed then,
you would be able to find the savior!
If you would not have the greed then,
you would be able to seek His glance!
If you would not have the greed then,
you would have real profitable deed!
If you would not have the greed then,
you would have real happiness of life!
If you would not have the greed then,
you would never be going to wrong!
If you would not have the greed then,
you would be not be indulged in lust!
But now just because of your greed,
never paid heed to do a good deed!
Now the time to audit has come and
He will look upon what you did so far!

64th Year

At sixty four year of age, it is time to pray,
but you are still on wrong path to decay!
Child to youth and then became matured,
black to white still not thought to cured!
You stop collecting more and more wealth,
because it will not go with and ruin health!
You are little away from the box of wood,
stop doing bad and start doing the good!
Still time to find sailor, strong boat to sail,
that take you away and save from whale!
Shut lusty eyes, don't look wives of others,
give them respect as sisters and mothers!
No one is going along with you oh my dear,
when time will come, no one may be near!
You have time to make strategy to amend,
to make amendment for profitable trend!
Start going to Church and obey the priest,
still time become human, you wild beast!

65th Year

At sixty five of age, it is time to be awake,
why indulged in the decor and to make!
Thinking of nice and bright cloths to wear,
but you are going away from the creator!
Stop ear-biting and saying bad for others,
treat woman as sister and him as brother!
God becomes happy with the good deeds,
and will become angry by the bad deeds!
Profit will come for sure with God's grace,
you will be blessed regardless of the race!
While trying and dipping in the Holy water,
must clean yourself, and become smarter!
Must make spiritual connections with God,
because He is savior and the ultimate Lord!
Remember you won't get human life again,
so do your every best to save from pain!
He to be good husband, she be good wife,
you carry on to enjoy this rare human life!

66th Year

In sixty six year age, you need to be wise,
soon your life will be ending and demise!
You are continuing to gain more n more,
keep in mind that He may shut His door!
Still inclined towards the false pleasures,
you may be deprived off, to His treasures!
Fit of ego and proud, not behaving as wise,
won't be able to escape, when time arise!
Be polite and sweet, while talk to others,
you don't become taker, better be giver!
Treat your life as a journey to this world,
don't hurt other, always use sweet word!
Now if you want to be loved by others,
treat everyone as sisters and brothers!
Good remain silent as they are in content,
those who just pretend will have to repent!
Be a humble person and don't have proud,
God will love you and keep in His heaven!

67th Year

In sixty seven years, start to love others,
as our father is one and we are brothers!
Remember if you love, you will be loved,
and if you save others, you will be saved!
As measure others, you will be measured,
if you donate then you will be treasured!
Do to make a sense, don't be nonsense,
you will be welcomed, if have patience!
He has given you tongue to speak sweet,
a good heart and gesture just to greet!
Those don't love others are far from Him,
but who obey are always dear to Him!
Good are those, who don't curse other,
they are winners in heaven, my brother!
He will be angry, if don't welcome a birth,
for children are Gifts of God, at the earth!
Don't hate others for love own's region,
treat equal to all, be faithful to religion!

68th Year

Now sixty eight age, don't play bluff,
don't be dull, become wise enough!
Wife is a human, give her good treat,
she take care of all, always in sweet!
She is best, let money handled by wife,
she will manage and make happy life!
If you don't have to pay off any debt,
your life is good, happy and the best!
Good are those who to other don't hate,
those who treat equal all, are great!
A person should be good in his deed,
even in business, at work or a creed!
If any person eat work hard of others,
will be answerable to God, my brother!
A person who always respect mothers,
won't be troubled at all by the others!
Person who has never been convicted,
will be loved by Him, heaven admitted!

69th Year

In sixty nine years, start loving others,
father, mother, sisters and brothers!
Power is gone and now you are weak,
will be rolled away in water of creek!
Tree of life, given by Him was powerful,
with bad deeds no leaves, now is dull!
Solid body was like of metal or brass,
now is broken bracelet made of glass!
The life is just like the ocean's waves,
that after heights have to go graves!
Ruined in false proud, ego and drama,
just like in intoxication of marijuana[1]!
All glitters will fade away very soon,
after the fortnight, won't see Moon!
Will not be always a king with crown,
remember that you have to fell down!
Your death will come in any moment,
still is time to start worship the God!

---

[1] **Marijuana:** Intoxicating drug

70th Year

Seventy years of age, no more a hero,
for your power has become near zero!
You will not be able to work anymore,
at the fields just because of no power!
You have sat down just like a traveler,
who travelled a lot and now has tired!
Power will be mixed in air, never to stay,
like smell of perfume has faded away!
Your lust and ego had not came to end,
will discarded by own, need to mend!
Your head was full of pride with crown,
now started shaking and came down!
Your own don't recognize and stopped,
though you raised, and they stepped!
If you had worshipped Lord, somehow,
you would have not faced all this now!
Still you have time to become a wise,
for that you should not be in duress!

71st Year

Seventy one year, still you are absurd,
don't know reason, why in this world!
Just holding book, no need to pretend,
read and apply in life, need to amend!
Reality, you have completely forgotten,
shortened life and became near rotten!
Bad deeds entries are in God's ledger,
to see, almighty Lord, won't pleasure!
He has given you just shape of Himself,
but why you have made, evil yourself!
All the times you continued to snatch,
by using your power and a bad catch!
You have completely forgotten Lord,
became thankless to Almighty God!
You don't pretend, a physician's zeal,
as you aren't knowledgeable to heal!
Why going away from purpose of life,
still have time, take care of yourself!

72nd Year

In seventy two years, you have taken,
wrong meaning of life, made shaken!
Now you are becoming weak and dim,
still won't be difficult to walk to Him!
Though tried to do best, to get access,
by forgetting Him, turned out useless!
Already have ruined the life, in amuse,
remember that all of this is of no use!
You did all bad towards innocent other,
and never respected father or mother!
All times you spoke bad, never sweet,
and remember, you won't be at greet!
Now you becoming weak, not to gain,
if you repent later, that will be in vain!
You will repent like peacock's[1] athlete,
cry after dance, looking the ugly feet!
Still got time to wake up and be wise,
otherwise later you will be too late!

---

[1]   **Peacock:** As per belief a peacock, after dancing start weeping
in tears after looking at his ugly feet (See page 123)

73rd Year

Now your seventy third year at a sake,
don't keep on sleeping, time to wake!
Beautiful youth now started to, diminish,
daylight will be gone, let noon be finish!
You life is like wood, which is unfinished,
will look better, if it is properly polished!
You deliberately fell down in the deep,
if you were blind of eyes, walking creek!
Neither you come out of worldly thirst,
nor left your false proud, ego and lust!
Around were good teachers and priest,
you never liked them from your heart!
You wasted your time and not reviewed,
you never did good, rather you deceived!
Neither you thought of opening the lock,
nor the wisdom and spiritualism, oh folk!
Now you would not be a powerful horse,
one day you have to be weak, of course!

74th Year

In seventy four, but not thought at all,
huge is already gone, left very small!
You spoiled precious life in fake trend,
remember, soon life is coming to end!
For sure won't last longer, this amuse,
will be audited and don't have excuse!
Now you are doing, all the bad deeds,
just for the fun, sure was not of needs!
All you did at a max extent, unwanted,
never bothered to listen, bells chanted!
You pretended an educated, a fake treat,
inside you are nothing except wild beast!
Even the used cloths, were not donated,
and good deed, you have just cremated!
By worshipping the idols, time is wasted,
never thought of Him who had created!
Still you have time and must be careful,
mend your ways, to face almighty God!

75th Year

At seventy five years, three fourth gone,
tell if you got wisdom, don't be a moan!
Tell the truth if you gained anything at all,
you spoiled three fourth and left is small
All times you spoke useless, never sweet,
and not worshipped Him, who will greet!
Always climbed to top, not thought at all,
humble is the best and pride has to fall!
You are eating delicious fruits and food,
but feeding an unfed, was never in mood!
The hard will be crushed into the powder,
the almighty will never welcome prouder!
Your beautiful body that kept in perfumed,
nice fragrance won't last, will be finished!
Remember, He always opposes the proud,
and is graceful to them those are humble!
Without faith you can't leave proud or ego,
must believe His existence, before you go!

76th Year

Now the seventy six years, is ready to own,
you might have seen many crops fell down!
You still not thought of worshiping the God,
and always got engaged in doing the odd!
You always kept busy taking care of other,
they won't share your sorrows, my brother!
Did maximum bad, destroyed your own life,
but never got time for good, will be in grief!
Never thought breaths will be ending soon,
You won't be able to enjoy Sun and Moon!
No one to clean the carpet and spread rug,
when time will come, then no one will hug!
Donating to the needy, was never clicked,
pretend to nice, but inside you just wicked!
Stop your ego and so called pride of mouth,
lust has not gone, even no more in a youth!
You do not be in hallucination that of a day,
open your eyes and see now it is time to lay!

78th Year

In seventy eight, do not make life sour,
do good now, it is a need of the hour!
No one knows the color[1] in stomach,
why becomes white or black, at out!
Stop collecting more and more wealth,
more wealth bring worries for health!
Slow and steady wins race, stop speed,
and don't differentiate, race or creed!
He is everlasting and never fade my dear,
because He is present here and there!
But cannot be described, has no shape,
dumb can't speak taste of sweet cake!
He is present at Church and at Temple,
he is everywhere, in house and jungle!
Whosoever wants to be with the Lord,
have to remember and pray the God!
He knows everything and in essence,
because of powerful Omni Presence!

---

[1]   **Color:** Here the word color means race or religion

79th Year

In seventy nine years, still sleeping,
if don't wake, later will be weeping!
Black turned to white is indication,
he is calling you by this invitation!
Now you cannot see with your eye,
soon will be unable move and cry!
You did many sins, please wake up,
later it will be hard for to make up!
If noting will go along, why to fight,
must do whatever is good and right!
Why you calculate, if weak in math,
dip in the water and take Holy bath!
Breaths stock is over, empty is drum
why you always pretend of wisdom!
Wore clean cloth, never cleaned self,
ignored priests to enlighten yourself!
Dear, still have time to worship God,
later you will be late to please Lord!

80th Year

Eighty years, you don't had wisdom,
and just spoiled your life doing odd!
The real profit lies in doing good act,
seems to do bad, you got a contract!
You spend your life, shopping in mall,
and you never tried to worship at all!
Whenever was asked, you done lols,
and instead, you went many idols!
From inside you are just like a devil,
who instead of right, has done evil!
You like to be called, saint of God,
but did nothing in name of Lord!
You always spoke wrong to other,
in name of God, killed many poor!
Knowing the truth that life is short,
never engaged in thought of God!
Those who are in worship of God,
and obey will never come to end!

81th Year

Now eighty first years is credited,
but never thought of to be audited!
You spoiled your life in just eating,
the hard earned sweats of others!
Your mind's horse is running fast,
try to hold the lead or will be lost!
You enjoyed everything at the max,
now is time to stop and just relax!
Remember, have to go very soon,
will be in a dark, no Sun or Moon!
All books are for here to remain,
if not read or applied, all in vain!
Wealth and forts will remain here,
just credit of worship to go there!
How long you will escaping deep,
all of your action are at His peep!
Remember won't successful at all,
in your mission if not worship Him!

82nd Year

Now you entered year eighty two,
still not thought life is short too!
When came on earth was a pure,
and has become evil for endure!
A big part of life is spent in pride,
and gap from Him is now at wide!
Still time stop all this nonsense,
for you won't be in repentance!
Since a long, enough pretended,
now is time, the ways to mend!
Now is good time, use your brain,
if want to be escaped from rain!
Wealth will not go along, is a fact,
then why you are busy in collect!
Now you have a choice to elect,
either God or wealth to collect!
In priest's rob, sowing bad seed,
be aware, He is looking at deed!

83rd Year

In your eighty three years age,
still you have not got wisdom!
White hair are grown all over,
became powerless and weak!
Why the world has forgotten,
almighty, who created this all?
All created by Him, are same,
why you differentiate in them?
You must worship the one but,
went others, who told you this?
Why you have not got rid of the,
difference of own and others?
Why importance and virtues of
real life, have been discarded?
How you can become a good,
until do not leave bad deeds?
Still time, not to spoil your life,
stop idolism, just accept Him!

84th Year

In eighty four still not listening,
to priests or saints[1] of the God!
Being a deaf, you are unable to,
listen, what they are teaching!
They can take you across river,
safely even without any boat!
They can show you right path,
to treat others equal and par!
They can give you a new torch,
which can turn dark into light!
What if they look like a poor,
they have all riches of the God!
Even the king bow their head,
for they are connected to God!
Take Holy Water[2] from them,
if want to get rid of your sins!
You need to listen teachings,
and go the way to salvation!

---

[1]   **Saints:** Means Priests
[2]   **Holy Water:** Blessed water with prayer.

85th Year

In eighty five years of your age,
now it is time to become a wise!
Time to think of your white hairs,
start worshiping Lord right now!
Dawn and noon are almost gone,
now dark has knocked at the door!
Being weak, if you slip or fell down,
become a point of laugh and fun!
Now you have lost all the respect,
your own have started to hate!
They created problems and fight,
for wealth, because got enough!
Whom you used to feed at first,
now gave you whatever is left!
Time to stop the fake relations,
that wait for insurance claims!
You need to stop kissing them,
and revert back love to Lord!

86th Year

Eighty six years age, you must stop,
your greed to get more and more!
Whom you used to give milk to drink,
are not giving you a glass of water!
You daughter-in-law is not only rude,
but has stood for revolt against you!
She is now trying her best to get over,
control of the house, that you made!
Earlier you were in control of the all,
now are being deprive of everything!
Earlier you were giving pocket money,
to them, now you are begging for it!
Now no one respect you anymore and
you are just helpless lying on the bed!
Everyone is thinking to replace the old,
and are throwing out your belongings!
Everyone is in search of the same age
companion, not the old one like you!

87th Year

In eighty seven years age still you,
have not thought of being wise!
You have collected all the wealth,
remember, will not go with you!
You build and they will destroy,
only this is reality of this world!
The powerful body will be buried,
and will be eaten by earth worms!
A pigeon who is singing in the joy,
is unaware of the bullet of hunter!
Today you are wandering in world,
but tomorrow, you will have to go!
One day your soft body will melt,
soon like banana lying in kitchen!
Your fate has come to sharp knife,
soon you will be cut into pieces!
Open your eyes and look around,
this world is just like a journey!

88th Year

In eighty eight years, still your
brain is empty of the wisdom!
You have never thought of God,
your life has been just wasted!
You are struggling at your best,
but you are nothing without God!
Why you are looking for Almighty,
at different places, just go to one!
If looking for Him in the jungles,
you will find wild beasts there!
If looking Him by outward baths,
you may get fishes nothing else!
Why you look Him just outside,
He is in good deeds, inside you!
He is available only to those, who
are sure and determined to find!
Remember He may put a tough,
examination before He meet you!

Remember gold gets shine only,
after passing through the fire!
Dry fruits become herbal to heal,
only and only after bearing heat!
Cloth look good, without wrinkle,
only after bearing the hot iron!
Will become winner, if work hard,
and don't leave it until finished!
Keep in mind that it is not easy,
to find the God, toward your side!

89th Year

Eighty ninth year, you havn't understood,
what is reality of human's birth and life!
If want to know the truth, read Holy Book,
stop immediately going to idols worship!
Stop murmuring, like a mad person who,
never keep of secret what he has gained!
You always remained in the false egoism,
and didn't thought, nothing will be yours!
You always appraised and enjoyed wrong,
never escaped from all these bad deeds!
Now you are wearing sober white cloths,
but still your thoughts are black inside!
You might have beaten drums for good,
actually, you never became good inside!
You are teaching others to be religious,
in reality you never became yourself!
You always worshipped idols in vain,
who never shown path to salvation!

90th Year

In ninetieth year, forgot cause, why you came,
but your time is running just like a ACE train[1]!
Now you are weak to walk, talk or to shower,
and just repenting for the days when in power!
The gone are the days of show off and shine,
be ready now like a guest, may go any time!
Life is like falling tree, at the edge of a river,
roots became naked with flowing of water!
The days of world tours are almost gone,
now lying on death bed of a nursing home!
Why looking at the Alzheimer's ward door,
for kids got wealth, won't come any more!
Remember, no one is coming to see or greet,
for you discarded, when they want to meet!
Yes spouse may come, if ever paid a heed,
not escaped, when spouse was in a need!
If was faithful to family, never ran away,
at least spouse will come, before decay!

---

[1]   **ACE Train:** A regional rail service in California

91st Year

In ninety one age, you are unable to take walk,
your lips are trembling and you can't even talk!
Now you don't have place to stay in your home,
for power will be ruler and timid to be thrown!
Now you lying in bed under care of a physician,
the days are gone when you were a musician!
Still holding the things around, more and more,
as these are yours and will have them forever!
All you have collected enough here and there,
by doing bad deed, are just going to stay here!
Your life's ticket finished, journey came to end,
still doing bad and have not thought to mend!
Now be ready for your last trip towards God,
how you will be taken, you do not know mod!
You were well aware to face the end, of course,
now won't be listened and thrown out by force!
There will be your trial, Judge will look at deeds,
He may grant you Heaven, if ever paid a heed!

92nd Year

In ninety two year age you still rubbing fist,
you went to others and forgot the real gist!
Now you have to do is control ego and pride,
as you do not have much time left your side!
You have lost the power and became weak,
unable to listen, speak or to have eat steak!
Time to leave lust, pride and getting more,
because now, His guards arrived at the door!
Almighty is great, you never ever had a nod,
but still have not started worshipping God!
Still become awake and stop tears to shed,
start reading Holy Book, while lying in bed!
Now unable to move and eyes became dim,
alas! you don't know how to get along Him!
It is easy to dressed up as advice of a priest,
wearing robs won't work, if drink and feast!
By going to others and idols, you will be dart,
will be greeted, if love Him from core of heart!

93rd Year

Ninety three year of age, but still not wise,
the black hair became white and has a rise!
A bigger portion of your life has been theft,
and now only a small portion of it has left!
Even in old age, if worshipped and got stick,
the doors of heaven, are opened very quick!
Like a dirty cloth if washed gives much glair,
your soul will also shine, if cleaned with care!
All jury has been instructed and ready to deal,
His decision will be prejudiced and no appeal!
Pending since a long, case file is big and wide,
Judge got evidences and now ready to decide!
Your deed were bad, now be ready to face fire,
also for the reason, you forgot Him to admire!
Your punishment will be hard, won't be ease,
because you do not have merits in your case!
All human must keep in mind, it is not any lie,
that whosoever is born, one day has to die!

94th Year

Now ninety four year of age has come,
but still you have not remembered Him!
Why you are now crying all the time and
why weep in tears, for lost time in vain!
Still time to worship Him leaving behind
the repenting, that may further delaying!
Now is the end time so leave your pride,
and be wise and faithful to obey the God!
You are thrown at the healthcare facility,
and your own have occupied your house!
You are on food, prescribed by physician,
not any choice of delicious food anymore!
Now you are given just used ironed cloths,
No shiny, costly clothes to wear anymore!
Gone is time you were ruling your house,
now have been already thrown out of it!
Now you see with your eyes their faces,
whom you used to loved much in regime!

95th Year

Since ninety five year age has come so
you need to start doing good to others!
It is time to donate the wealth to others,
for a fact that nothing will go along you!
Time has come, to get a rid of medicines,
for fact that these won't hold you at all!
Give all of grain and food you have now,
because soon you will have to go to God!
Meet your near and dear, as much as can,
because soon you will have to leave them!
Now is time stop looking at other female,
because soon, you will depart your own!
Your children, their spouses and the kids,
now will enjoy the mansion you had made!
Remember, whosoever is born has to die,
now their blessings or wishes won't work!
Still you are warned, be involve with God,
That is only way and that is it should be!

96th Year

It is ninety six year of age,
remember you have to go!
Soon the bird will fly away,
as cage has become an old!
Eyes and brain came to end,
and you are helpless now!
Your boat to Him is ready,
sailor started calling you!
To punish you for the bad,
His cops are arrived now!
Grains and produce stock,
is finished, you have to go!
Your final destination is,
same where came from!
Any day or any moment,
can happen anything now!
You, must be ready now,
and must be ready to go!

97th Year

In ninety seven year age,
your head start shaking!
Eyes has stopped seeing,
ears has stopped to hear!
The bright face no more,
all you have is ugly face!
Light is now gone almost,
and the dark is all around!
Organs stopped working,
like robbers robbed you!
Since never worshipped,
you are the enemy of self!
Body is ready to be out,
have afraid of the ghost!
You don't have any space,
in the heaven with Him!
Just because of your deeds
And just because of deeds!

98th Year

At ninety eight years,
end time is very near!
You can't swim and,
boat is ready to sink!
Only a little has left,
the major has gone!
Breaths are no more,
like someone stolen!
Last time has come,
be ready to fell down!
You never did good,
now will be in coffin!
Just lay on the berth,
and be mixed in earth!
He will look at yours,
causes to award you!
If were bad then Hell
if good then Heaven!

99th Year

Ninety nine year age,
your end time is near!
The tree has become,
old and ready to cut!
Breaths came to end,
like gambler has lost!
You never did good,
bad time is coming!
Your age is finished,
and spent in wrong!
You lost your times,
enjoying pleasures!
If not did any noble,
now you will repent!
You are at the target,
of the hunter's shot!
The train has whistled,
it is time to ride now!

100th Year

Century's bell has rang for your death,
you are out of granted stock of breath!
His messengers came to take from earth,
and soon you will be put on the berth!
Now that They[1] are standing at the door,
they will shut it to take you to the Lord!
Your coffin is ready and be ready to lay,
no more shine, now it is time to decay!
You will be evaluated and be audited,
for good or bad, to be rightly awarded!
You have consumed all that you worth,
time to say good bye and leave earth!

---

[1]   **They:** Messengers of the Almighty God

My Prayer To Readers!

On tenth of July of twenty thirteenth year,
I finished this life sketch of hundred year!
Being a human, not a poet, priest or Lord,
I did my best for the humanity and God!
But if you think, in writing I got a success,
then three are behind its writing process!
One who raised and second for education,
and third one for brining God's revelation!
I hope readers by reading will understand,
and for my mistakes, they will not mind!
Because, with wisdom I got from my God,
completed this first book for my own lord!
Proceeds of this will be used for new title,
noble cause to write a New Punjabi Bible!

Bibliography

1. Biography.com for various biographies of celebrities
2. Conway-Gomez & others for Malthus Theory article
3. Google.com Google Inc. as main source for search
4. Library.thinkquest.org for various type search info
5. Nikeinc.com about details of Nike Inc. USA products
6. Preservearticles.com for The Wolf and Lamb Story
7. Shri Sadhu Daya Singh for his creation Jindagibilas
8. Speakingtree.in for important Taj Mahal Imp info
9. Tahnee Hopman for Ravana King of Sri Lanka article
10. Tajmahal.org.uk/mumtaz-mahal.html for Taj Mahal
11. Thefreedictionary.com for various meaning and search
12. Thewhiskyexchange.com for Civas regal whiskey info
13. Urbandictionary.com for various meaning and search
14. Wikipedia.org for biographies and other research
15. Holy Bible (NIV) by International Bible Society, USA
16. The Holy Bible in the King James Version
17. Dake's Annotated Reference Bible, by Bookmark, USA

Appendix

Abraham Lincoln

Abraham Lincoln was the President of the United States. He led the United States through its greatest constitutional, military and strengthening the national government and modernizing the economy. Reared in a poor family, he was self-educated who worked hard and became 16th President of United States.

Akbar The Great

Born on October 15, 1542 at Umarkot, India, and enthroned at age 14, Akbar the Great began his military conquests under the tutelage of a regent before claiming imperial power and expanding the Mughal Empire. Known as much for his inclusive leadership style as for his war mongering, Akbar ushered in an era of religious tolerance and appreciation for the arts. Akbar the Great died in 1605.

Blue

The use of the word "blue" to refer to sexually explicit content was first recorded in Scotland in 1824. "Blue" meant "lewd" because prostitutes dressed in blue gowns. Blue movie a Jamaican phrase used to describe porn. Blue movies that give you boners when you watch them, but you are in the theatre so you can't do anything about it unless you want to become a peewee hermon.

Boudica

Boudica, also known as Boadicea, was from a Celtic tribe who led an uprising against the occupying forces of the Roman Empire in AD 60 or 61. At her husband's death, Boudica was flogged and her daughters were raped by the Romans.

While the Roman governor Gaius Suetonius Paulinus was leading a campaign on the island of Anglesey off the northwest coast of Wales, Boudica led 100,000 Iceni, Trinovantes and others to fight the Legio IX Hispana and burned and destroyed Londinium, Verulamium. An estimated 70,000-80,000 Romans and British were killed in the three cities by those led by Boudica and she resecured Roman control of the province.

Chivas Regal

The blend for grown-ups, for people who have made their rites of passage and are ready to enjoy their success. Sweet, but not cloying. Buxom, but not overblown.

George I

George I was born on May 28, 1660, in Osnabrück, Hanover to the elector of Hanover. He succeeded his father in 1697. When his mother, the granddaughter of King James I of England, died, he inherited the throne. He was part of the Whig Party, but was not popular in England. He forged an alliance with France, but narrowly escaped disgrace for questionable investments. He died of a stroke in 1727.

Ghost

In traditional belief and fiction, a ghost or phantom, or spook is the soul or spirit of a dead person or animal that can appear, in visible form or other manifestation, to the living. Descriptions of the apparition of ghosts vary widely from an invisible presence to translucent or barely visible wispy shapes, to realistic, lifelike visions.

The belief in manifestations of the spirits of the dead is widespread, dating back to animism or ancestor worship in pre-literate cultures. Ghosts are generally described as solitary essences that haunt particular locations, objects, or people they were associated with in life, though stories of phantom armies, ghost trains, phantom ships, and even host animals have also been recounted.

Henry VII of Germany
Born in 1211, in Sicily, Henry VII, son of emperor Frederick II, was crowned king of his home state at the age of 1. He became German king by the early 1220s, though, amidst geopolitical instability, he would eventually join with the Lombard League in an uprising against his father during the 1230s. Henry was captured and later imprisoned in Calabria, where he died on February 12, 1242.

Henry Ford
Henry Ford (1863-1947) was an American industrialist, the founder of the Ford Motor Company, and sponsor of the development of the assembly line technique of mass production. Ford did not invent the automobile, but he developed and manufactured the first automobile that many middle class Americans could afford to buy. As owner of the Ford Motor Company, he became one of the richest and best-known people in the world. His intense commitment to

systematically lowering costs resulted in many technical and business innovations, including a franchise system that put dealerships throughout most of North America and in major cities on six continents. Ford left most of his vast wealth to the Ford Foundation and arranged for his family to control the company permanently.

Herod
Herod, later known as Herod the Great, became king over Judea. He was the king that the wise men of the east spoke concerning the birth of the King of the Jews. Herod was upset, and inquired of the chief priests where Christ was to be born. Herod then sent the Magi to Bethlehem, feigning the wish to also come and worship the new king. After the wise men saw the young child, they were warned not to return to Herod. Herod, learning that the men from the east had fled, was enraged. He sent out his soldiers to slaughter all male children two years old and under in Bethlehem and the surrounding neighborhoods. (Matthew 2:1-4, 7, 16) After ruling for about 37 years, Herod died at Jericho about 4 B.C.

Hitler, Adolf
Born in Austria in 1889, Adolf Hitler rose to power in German politics as leader of the National Socialist German Workers Party, also known as the Nazi Party. Hitler was chancellor of Germany from 1933 to 1945, and served as dictator from 1934 to 1945. His policies precipitated World War II and the Holocaust. Hitler committed suicide with wife Eva Braun on April 30, 1945, in his Berlin bunker.

Malthusian Theory of Population

Thomas Robert Malthus was the first economist to propose a systematic theory of population. In Essay on the Principle of Population, Malthus proposes the principle that human populations grow exponentially. The scenario of his arithmetic food growth with simultaneous geometric human population growth predicted a future when humans would have no resources to survive on.

On the basis of a hypothetical Malthus suggested that there was a potential for a population increase to 256 billion within 200 years but that the means of subsistence were only capable of being increased enough for nine billion to be fed at the level prevailing at the beginning of the period.

He saw positive checks to population growth as being any causes that contributed to the shortening of human lifespans. He included in this category poor living and working conditions which might give rise to low resistance to disease, as well as more obvious factors such as disease itself, war, and famine. Some of the conclusions that can be drawn from Malthus's ideas thus have obvious political connotations and this partly accounts for the interest in his writings and possibly also the misrepresentation of some of his ideas by authors such as Cobbett, the famous early English radical. Others did not accept the view that birth control should be forbidden after marriage, and one group in particular, called the Malthusian League, strongly argued the case for birth control, though this was contrary to the principles of conduct which Malthus himself advocated.

Mughal

The Mughal Dynasty was the last great empire of Indian history. Such was their greatness that not only did they leave a lasting impact on Indian history, the English word Mogul (derived from Mughal) means a powerful person. The Mughals were a remarkable dynasty, and at their peak they produced a successive set of capable rulers. It was also during their reign that some of the finest monuments of India were built, most notably one of the seven wonders of the world, the Taj Mahal.

The Mughal dynasty was founded by Babur, who was a ruler of a kingdom near Persia (modern day Iran). Babur had long cherished a desire to conquer India. He first conquered Afghanistan and then descended into India. In just half a day, he captured Delhi and its surrounding areas. The Mughal empire was not firmly established in his time, in fact shortly after his son Humayun succeeded him, Sher Shah, temporarily threw out the Mughal power and set up his own empire. Upon his death however Humayun returned and re-established the Mughal empire. The greatest Mughal king, Akbar followed and he took the empire to its peak. When we talk of the Mugahl empire we usually refer to the reign of the greater Mughals: Babur, Humayaun, Akbar, Jehangir, Shah Jehan and Aurangzeb. The Mughal empire began to disintegrate during the reign of Aurangzeb and the Mughal emperors after him are collectively referred to as the later Mughals. The Mughal empire would be an important part of Indian history for the next two hundred years, before its disintegration would pave the way for the rise of the British in India.

Mumtaz Mahal

Shah Jahan who built the Taj Mahal, a wondrous monument built in dedication to love, beauty, and life of Mumtaz Mahal, had succeeded in his lifetime his dire wish to immortalize the name of Mumtaz Mahal, his third wife. Such is the esteem of Mumtaz Mahal that she is known by one and all, who've ever heard of Taj Mahal.

Born in 1593 as Arjumand Banu Begum, Mumtaj Mahal was the daughter of Abdul Hasan Asaf Khan and a princess from the Persian nobility. She was so beautiful that Shah Jahan (then Prince Khurram) fell in love with her at the first sight. It was in 1607 that she was betrothed to Prince Khurram and soon became the unquestionable love of his life.

Five years later in 1612, their marriage was solemnized. Although she was one of the three wives of Shah Jahan, she was his favorite. He even bestowed her with the name Mumtaz Mahal meaning "Jewel of the Palace", and the highest honor of the land—the royal seal, Mehr Uzaz.

Mumtaz Mahal had a very deep and loving marriage with Shah Jahan. Even during her lifetime, poets would extol her beauty, gracefulness and compassion. She was his trusted companion and traveled with him all over the Mughal Empire. It is believed that she was the perfect wife and portrayed no aspirations of political power. Apart from counseling and supporting her husband, and playing the role of a lovable wife to Emperor Shah Jahan. She died in 1631, while giving birth to their 14th child, and left for the holy abode.

Shah Jahan loved Mumtaj Mahal so much that he decided to build the world's richest mausoleum in memory of his Jewel, i.e. Mumtaz. It took 22 years and most of his royal treasury to build a monument befitting the memory of his beloved wife. Now, in the name of Mumtaz Mahal stands the most beautiful building in the universe and that monument of love, purity and unparalleled beauty is called the Taj Mahal.

Newton

Sir Isaac Newton was an English physicist and mathematician who is widely regarded as one of the most influential scientists of all time and as a key figure in the scientific revolution.

Newton formulated the laws of motion and universal gravitation that dominated scientists' view of the physical universe for the next three centuries. It also demonstrated that the motion of objects on the Earth and that of celestial bodies could be described by the same principles.

Newton built the first practical reflecting telescope and developed a theory of color based on the observation that a prism decomposes white light into the many colors of the visible spectrum. He also formulated an empirical law of cooling and studied the speed of sound.

Newton was a fellow of Trinity College and the second Lucasian Professor of Mathematics at the University of Cambridge. In his later life, Newton became president of the Royal Society. He also served the British government as Warden and Master of the Royal Mint.

Nike

Dictionery meaning of nike is an ancient Greek goddess of victory. However in USA, Nike, Inc. is an American multinational corporation that is engaged in the design, development and worldwide marketing and selling of footwear, apparel, equipment, accessories and services.

Parrot and Beetle Story

As per the story narrated by my father, once upon a time a parrot met a creed while eating a sweet fruit in a garden. Parrot helped the little beetle with some food and both became friends. Many time parrot gave the beetle ride under his feathers and used to take him to different delicious fruit tree and both used to enjoy together. After many months passed, one day parrot desired to see the house of little beetle. At the creed's residence parrot unknowingly asked something to eat. The beetle, who used to eat poisonous herb fruits, hesitated and showed his inability to provide food. But when, parrot insisted, he gave him his usual food. As parrot put his bill in the fruit, a poison's drop feel into his eyes and he became blind on the spot and thus ruined his life also. By telling this story, my father used to teach me that always have friendship with good people so that you should not put yourself in danger or to a great loss.

Peacock's Cry

A beautiful peacock with multicolor feathers is treated as bird of paradise. God expelled peacock from heaven because of its bad deed and as a curse God gave him ugly feet so that it should remember his bad deed. In order to please peahen (female peacock), peacock start dancing but as its dance is over it looks at feet and cry out because his feet are no beautiful at all. In other words, it reminds him his mistake and he assumed to feel guilt and cries out.

Rama A Hindu Diety

Rama is the seventh avatar of the God Vishnu in Hinduism, and a king of Ayodhya in Hindu scriptures. Along with Krishna, the eighth avatar of Vishnu, Rama is considered to be the most important avatar of Vishnu. He is also one of the most popular gods in Hinduism and is widely worshipped throughout India and Nepal. In a few Rama-centric sects,

Rama is considered the Supreme Being, rather than an avatar. Rama was born in Suryavansha later known as Raghuvansha and his father was also a king known by the name of Dashratha.

Ravana

The Ravana was a great king of Sri Lanka. In ancient time, Sri Lanka was also known by the name of Ceylon. As per Ramayana a great Hindu Epic, he kidnapped the wife of Hindu diety, Rama. He was very proudy and refused to return back Sita (wife of Rama). Thus he ruined his whole nation in a historical fight with King and Hindu Lord Rama.

Taj Mahal

The Taj Mahal is known for its aesthetic look and wonderful design. It is the monument of India, attracts countless visitors around the globe. People all over the world desire to see the grandeur of the Taj Mahal and only a lucky few get to see this wonder in marble. The world class monument, one of most flawless architectural creations of world forced people to see its incomparable beauty. It signifies and glorifies human love, has withstood the test of time, and still stands in all its glory.

The construction of this marble masterpiece is credited to the Mughal emperor Shah Jahan who constructed it in the memory of his beloved wife Mumtaj Mahal. This was because, her last wish to her husband was to build a tomb in her memory such as the world had never seen before. The master piece is now among the Seven Wonders of the World.

The famous Golden Triangle of India actually covers three most beautiful and captivating cities of the country Delhi, Agra and Jaipur, the pink city. People desiring to visit this ultimate monument, often come with their families and friends.

Wolf and Lamb Story

Once upon a time a wolf went to a stream to quench his thirst with water. While he was drinking water, he saw a lamb that was also drinking water over there. At the sight of lamb, his mouth began to water. He turned to the lamb and said, "How dare you make the water muddy? Can't you see that I am drinking water from the same stream?"

The lamb got so much frightened that it could not speak for a while. Then it replied, "Sir, I beg your pardon. The water is running down from you to me. How can I make it muddy?" The wolf said, "But you bleated me and called me names last year" The lamb replied, "Sir, I was not even born then. How could I abuse you last year?"

The wolf, who was determined to eat the poor lamb, said to it, "Then it must have been your father or mother or brother. You must suffer for your race." Saying so, the wolf caught him, tore him to pieces and ate him up.

Wright Brothers
The Wright brothers, Orville (1871-1948) and Wilbur (1867-1912), were two American brothers, inventors, and aviation pioneers who were credited with inventing and building the world's first successful airplane and making the first controlled, powered and sustained heavier-than-air human flight, on December 17, 1903. From 1905 to 1907, the brothers developed their flying machine into the first practical fixed-wing aircraft

From the beginning of their aeronautical work, the Wright brothers focused on developing a reliable method of pilot control as the key to solving "the flying problem". Their first U.S. patent, 821,393, did not claim invention of a flying machine, but rather, the invention of a system of aerodynamic control that manipulated a flying machine's surfaces.

They gained the mechanical skills essential for their success by working for years in their shop with printing presses, bicycles, motors, and other machinery. Their work with bicycles in particular influenced their belief that an unstable vehicle like a flying machine could be controlled and balanced with practice.

Yoga
Yoga is a commonly known generic term for the physical, mental, and spiritual practices or disciplines which originated

in ancient India with a view to attain a state of permanent peace. Specifically, yoga is one of the six āstika ("orthodox") schools of Hindu philosophy. One of the most detailed and thorough expositions on the subject is the Yoga Sūtras of Patañjali, which defines yoga as "the stilling of the changing states of the mind". Yoga has also been popularly defined as "union with the divine" in other contexts and traditions. Various traditions of yoga are found in Hinduism.

Swami Vivekananda, brought yoga to the West in the late 19th century. In the 1980s, yoga became popular as a system of physical exercise across the Western world. Many studies have tried to determine the effectiveness of yoga as a complementary intervention for cancer, schizophrenia, asthma and heart patients.

Free Bible Project

All Proceeds and royalty of 100 Life Sketch (Christian Spiritual Journey) will be used towards FREE distribution of New Punjabi Bible to 4.5 million Punjabi Christians living in India. Translation work has already been in full swing under supervision of Prof. Somraj Arya. The New Punjabi Bible is need of an hour, so your donation and cooperation will be highly appreciated.

Make an impression for life!

Donate for this noble cause and make an impression among 4.5 million Christian Lives forever!

Top 25 donator's names will be published on the first page New Punjabi Bible. Names along with the amount of donations will be released to all donators before the printing of Bible.

Please make donation check payable to "God Believers Society USA" and mail to:

God Believers Society USA
P.O. Box 7422 Fremont,
CA 94537-7422 (USA)

NOTES

NOTES

NOTES

NOTES

NOTES

NOTES

NOTES